ANNA AIRY
(1882-1964)

The story of her life and work.
By Andrew Casey

Produced by The Ipswich Art Society, 2014,
to mark the 50th Anniversary of the
Anna Airy Award for young Suffolk artists,
and to commemorate Airy's achievements
as a war artist in the First World War

Published by Leiston Press
Printed by Print 4 U Ltd, Ipswich
Designed by Derek Chambers

ISBN No: 978-1-907938-77-1

CONTENTS

RIGHT:
Morning Sunlight, 1926,
oil on canvas, 61 x 74 cm, DMBC Doncaster Museum Service.

PREVIOUS PAGE:
Leopard Moth and Plums, c.1920,
watercolour, pen and ink, 39 x 47.5cm By kind permission of
Sarah Colegrave Fine Art, London.

FRONT COVER:
A period photograph of Anna Airy, probably 1920s.
By kind permission of Mr C. Lofts.

INSIDE COVER:
A period image of Anna Airy in her studio in Playford, Suffolk,
drawing a woman, probably 1920s.
By kind permission of Mr C. Lofts.

FOREWORD

This book has been created to celebrate the work, inspiration and life of Anna Airy. She was a serious and ambitious artist and a superb draughtsman, who had a long and successful career. There is a freshness and immediacy to her work which is impressive.

Anna Airy was one of the first women to be commissioned as a war artist during the First World War. She produced some of her most outstanding canvases for the Canadian and British authorities. Five magnificent paintings are in the collection of the Imperial War Museum.

Anna Airy also became the first woman President of the Ipswich Art Society in 1945. She was very influential in raising standards and in inspiring young artists to show their work. She continued as President for almost 20 years. The Anna Airy Award was set up by the Society soon after her death in 1964 to continue her work in encouraging and rewarding excellence in the work of young artists.

In recent years her work has been rather neglected, and it is hoped that this publication will help in bringing her work back to the attention it deserves. We at the Ipswich Art Society are very grateful to Andrew Casey for the research and writing and to Derek Chambers for the design and production of this beautiful book.

Judith Lockie, President, Ipswich Art Society

The Little Mirror,
oil on canvas, 122 x 81cm. Reproduced by kind permission of the Rehs Galleries Inc, New York.

CHAPTER ONE:
ANNA AIRY: MAKING A START IN ART

Anna Airy was one of only a few important and established women artists working in Britain during the early part of the 20th century. She was a versatile and gifted artist and mastered a variety of media including oil, watercolour and etching. Her subject matter was varied, including studies of people in interiors, plant forms and munitions' factories. Underpinning all her work was a determination to produce outstanding art. Many of those who knew her considered her to be one of the most gifted English women artists, yet she still remains relatively unknown compared to others, such as Laura Knight.

Her formidable character and adventurous spirit enabled her to break away from the artistic conventions of the period, tackle difficult situations and overcome the restrictions that were placed on her as a woman in a male-dominated world. Her indomitable spirit gave her the strength to develop her work and to undertake First World War commissions recording the process of manufacturing in an industrial setting. In 1933 Airy moved, with her husband, to the family home in Playford, Suffolk and in 1945 she was elected President of the Ipswich Art Club, a post she held for almost twenty years. Her achievements were celebrated at a special exhibition in London in 1952. The Foreword of the catalogue noted that, *"the basis of Anna Airy's art is this ability to observe, to reflect and to interpret."* [1]

Anna Airy was born into an illustrious and prosperous family in Greenwich, London, on June 6, 1882. Her grandfather, Sir George Biddell Airy, K.C.B., was Astronomer Royal at Greenwich from 1835 to 1881. Anna was the only child of engineer Wilfrid Airy and Anna (the daughter of Professor Listing of Gottingen). Her mother died two weeks after her birth, and Airy was raised by her two unmarried aunts, Annot and Christabel, in her grandfather's home. [2] As a gifted young girl Airy was unsure whether to choose art or music as a career and was encouraged by her aunts, both competent artists, to pursue art. Airy commented many years later that: *"I had an adorable father. He was very generous and very good, I can remember him saying to me that if I persisted in going in for art when I left school that he would give me the finest art*

education either in this country or on the Continent that could be had at the time, after which I must stand on my own two feet."* [3]

At the age of 17 Airy began her artistic studies at the Slade School of Fine Art in London, from 1899 to 1903. She worked under Frederick Brown, Henry Tonks, Professor of Art, School of Fine Art and Philip Wilson Steer, who taught painting. Although much younger, Airy was a contemporary of both Augustus John and William Orpen. Students were encouraged to develop good draughtsmanship, which is evident in her subsequent work. Airy must have made an impression amongst her fellow students, as she won the Melvill Nettleship Prize for figure drawing, for three years running. [4] Airy was also awarded the Professor Thane's prize for anatomy and the Slade School Scholarship in 1902. [5] She commented of her time at the Slade that: *"We were an enterprising lot, constantly on the look-out for fresh material for study. I - at eighteen or nineteen - was specially keen on seeing life in the raw! I got taken to some of the Thames-side haunts, between East Greenwich and Woolwich, to study human nature under slum conditions at first hand! I saw a prize fighter once - without gloves - in a warehouse, and won a sovereign which other people drank. And another time I saw a cock-fight. Once I got involved in a police sweep in connection with a mishap in a gambling den underground - a scene which I afterwards recorded in The Gambling Club. That was an exciting night."* [6]

After leaving the Slade, and probably with the financial support of her family, Airy set about establishing herself as a professional artist. She moved into her own studio: 7, The Studios, Sherriff Road, West Hampstead, in about 1905. Airy must have started to develop her own work very soon after leaving the Slade, as by the early part of the twentieth century she was able to build a collection of work ready to exhibit. In 1905 her oil painting *Michael Lee Esq.: Indian Mutiny* (1905) was accepted for the Summer Exhibition at the Royal Academy of Arts. A year later her *Willow Pattern* pen and wash drawing was shown and later exhibited at the Franco-British Exhibition in 1908. [7] Airy continued to exhibit every year until 1956, with the exception of 1931. Commenting on her early work, Martin Hardie noted: *"working on canvas in her early days she appears to have sought her method in the school of Velasquez and Hals, and she clearly appreciated the art of her contemporaries, Sargent and Brangwyn. That*

LEFT: A drawing of the Airy cottage thought to be by Richarda Biddell Airy, c.1840s.

Michael Lee Esq.-Indian Mutiny, 1905,
oil on canvas, 86.5 x118cm. Shown at the Royal Academy of Arts
Summer Exhibition in 1905. © Bonhams London, UK/The
Bridgeman Art Library

OPPOSITE TOP RIGHT:
Succory,
watercolour, pen and ink, 38 x 17cm, exhibited at the Fine Art
Society, London, in 1920
By kind permission of Sarah Colegrave Fine Art, London

LOWER RIGHT:
Error in Pay, 1918,
oil on canvas, 122 x 152cm, shown at
the Summer Exhibition of the Royal Academy of Arts in 1918

was a good beginning, but it meant that in her painting there was the long searching look followed by the bold sweep of the brush, the direct and never the niggling approach, the frontal attack rather than the cautious encirclement". 8

As her status as a professional artist grew, she joined a number of important societies in London including The Pastel Society in 1906, Royal Society of Painters and Etchers in 1914 and the Royal Institute of Painters in Watercolours in 1918.9 In 1907 Airy held her first one-woman show at the Carfax & Co. Gallery in London.10 This important exhibition, featuring paintings, drawings and etchings, brought her to the attention of the press, with one art critic regarding her as one of the most promising young female painters of her generation, noting that: *"she can paint, she can draw and she can etch."* 11

Airy, unlike many artists of that time, worked successfully in a wide range of media and for subject matter she employed a range of themes from still life studies to the natural world. Her exhibition at the Fine Art Society in 1920 featured a special exhibit: a collection of forty-six decorative panels depicting insects, entitled *The Bee's Rakes Progress*. The quality of her drawings and watercolours brought her great praise and coverage in magazines such as International Studio which carried a five-page article about her most recent work, illustrating six pieces including *The Wrong Label* and *The Split Quince*. They also described how the artist worked: *"Not a line is drawn by her except in the presence of nature. The pen work is done out of doors direct from the model branch as it grows on the tree, and the colouring is done in the same circumstances. A whole summer, with hours from six till sunset, has been spent in the orchard by the artist."* 12

In particular, she excelled in figure compositions, often telling a story or giving the viewer a snapshot of an incident, as typified by *The Gambling Club* (1913) or *Error in Pay* (1918). Interestingly, the artist was not inspired by the landscape as the subject for her work, although she acknowledged that she used it as settings for her favourite themes.13 To develop her work, she would often use local people or her own housekeeper and the village women from Playford, for example in *The Tale Bearer* (1915). Some of her larger works, such as *The Flower Shop* (1923), exhibited at the Royal Academy of Arts Summer Exhibition, required staging with props, models and floral displays. Airy commented: *"It was the biggest rig-up I ever had, and for the two months it took to paint, the whole place became a flower shop. I had a contract with a florist, who sent twice a week to bring new*

Willow Pattern, 1906,
71 x 66cm, watercolour and pen. Shown at the Royal Academy of Arts Summer Exhibition in 1906.

flowers and plants and to take away the old. As I soon found out, the flowers would change and droop from hour to hour indoors in the sunny weather. I had to work very quickly, and even took my meals at the easel to save time." [14]

Having successfully had work accepted at the Royal Academy of Arts Summer Exhibition for many years, alongside her contemporary female artists such as Flora Lion, Clara Atwood, Annie Swynnerton and Alice Fanner, questions started to be raised in the press concerning the lack of female Royal Academicians (RA) or Associates of the Royal Academy (ARA). To date only one woman had been elected to the position: Lady Butler. According to an article in the press the RA had, many years earlier, eliminated women from its constitution, therefore making women no longer eligible for election and not officially recognised. In response, *Queen* magazine suggested that these prolific women artists should get together and organise their own exhibition to demonstrate their artistic achievements. Laura Knight became the first fully elected woman at the RA in 1936. [15]

In 1916 Anna Airy married Geoffrey Buckingham Pocock, a fellow artist and well-known painter and teacher of etching. They had met during their time at the Slade. He showed his work at the Royal Academy of Arts Summer Exhibition for a number of years, specialising in landscapes. Having studied at the Slade, he later became life master at the London County Council School of Photo-Engraving and Lithography. Her marriage did not interrupt her career or tempt her to settle down and enjoy the sedate family life taken for granted by most Edwardian women of her class. In those days it was fashionable for established artists to spend time in Europe, especially in Paris, but Airy never left the country. The couple shared a studio at 5 Parkhill Road Studios, Haverstock Hill, which Airy had moved into in 1907. The studio was very plain, with two tall cabinets filled with sketches, etchings and prints, a flat pile of canvases with two easels and two high painting stools. The studio, which led into the garden, featured a skylight and two tall windows. A contemporary magazine commented: *"no feminine fripperies are here! Not a mirror, not a chandelier, not even a piece of drapery about - none of the familiar."* [16]

One of Anna Airy's most important achievements, and the one for which she is best remembered, was being one of the first women war artists during the First World War. In 1917 she was commissioned, alongside other

artists, to produce an art work for the Canadian War Memorials Fund Committee.

Her finished painting, entitled *Cook-house at Witley Camp*, depicted soldiers from the 156th Canadian Infantry Battalion. Towards the end of the First World War the Ministry of Information started to commission a wide range of British artists to record aspects of the war. As women were not allowed to go to the front, the Committee set up the locations for her to complete four large oil studies, representing typical scenes in munitions' factories around Britain. This commission was probably the most prestigious and challenging work that she had undertaken, not least because the Committee was very strict about canvas sizes, titles of work and deadlines. The first suggested names for these four works were: *Assembly Shop at the Aircraft Manufacturing Co., Hendon; The "L" press forging an 18" gun at the works of Messrs. Armstrong Whitworth & Co's. Works at Openshaw; 15" Shell Shop at Singer's, Glasgow; and The Shell Forge - Hackney Marshes, London.* Many years later the Ministry of Information commissioned further artists to record aspects of the Second World War but many of those First World War artists, including Airy, whilst still active, were rejected.[17]

During the 1930s and 1940s Airy continued to paint and exhibit her work. In 1933 she and her husband left London and moved to the family home in Playford, Suffolk, where she had previously spent a great deal of time. The house had been bought by her grandfather in the early 19th century as a retreat from London pollution and was eventually bequeathed to her following the death of her father in 1925. Airy commissioned a monument to her father and grandfather inside St Mary's Church in Playford. The Cottage, as it was known, featured a small studio where Airy worked, although she always preferred to work outside, capturing nature around her. Airy attended church every Sunday and otherwise kept herself to herself in the village.

Airy became involved with the Ipswich Fine Art Club (est. 1874) from the early 1920s when her work was accepted into the annual exhibition. Following her permanent move to Suffolk, Airy started to play a more important role within the Club. In 1943, at the Wolsey Gallery at Christchurch Mansion in Ipswich,

A painting of Playford Farm by Geoffrey Buckingham Pocock, oil on canvas, c. 1920s. By kind permission of Mr C. Lofts.

Airy held a special exhibition of her work. Within two years she was elected as President. This position gave her the opportunity to express her ideas about art and to endeavour to improve the standards of the work shown at the annual exhibition.[18] Airy was also very keen to encourage young people into the Club, having been a part-time inspector to the Board of Education. Her work was often illustrated in publications such as the Studio and the Colour magazine. She was also responsible for three publications: *The Art of Pastel* in 1930, *Making a Start in Art* in 1951 and *London Lyrics and Country Pieces*, 1940s.

In 1952, The Royal Society of British Artists held a special Jubilee exhibition honouring her great talent, entitled Anna Airy: Paintings, Drawings and Prints. The exhibition was opened by Sir Gerald Kelly, President of the Royal Academy of Arts. The show included *The Fledgling* (1932), *The Termagant* and *Heartbreak Stairs* (1928). This exhibition was important enough to warrant a whole page in the *London Illustrated News*, illustrating several of her works. In the same year Airy was invited to open the first Bradford Arts Club Jubilee exhibition.[19] Throughout her illustrious career her work was exhibited in museums and galleries in this country and abroad including Italy, Canada, New Zealand, Australia and the United States. Her work is held in several important galleries and museums including the British Museum, Victoria and Albert Museum and the Imperial War Museum. Her work is also held in the Royal Collection.

Anna Airy passed away on 23rd October 1964. Margaret Tempest, committee member of the Ipswich Art Club, (later known as Lady Mears) paid tribute to the late President, stating: *"it was agreed that during her twenty years of office she had done far more than could have been expected of any President, and that we shall never have another like her. She gave instinctively of her great knowledge and skill, especially in the selection and hanging of pictures and in her criticisms and demonstrations, and she guided and guarded us with great wisdom."* [20]

In recognition of her important contribution, Ipswich Art Club established the Anna Airy Award to promote the work of young artists aged between 16 and 20. In 1985 the Ipswich Art Club, in association with Ipswich Borough Council, presented a retrospective exhibition of her work at Christchurch Mansion, in Ipswich. This celebratory exhibition brought together many examples of the artist's work for the first time, including oil paintings, drawings, etchings, pastel work and examples of her First World War paintings.

FOOTNOTES:
1. Hardie, M., Foreword in the exhibition catalogue: *Anna Airy R.I., R.O.I., R.E. Paintings Drawings Prints*, RBA Galleries, 1952, p.1-2.
2. Three works by Christabel Airy were shown at the Retrospective Exhibition, *Anna Airy R.I., R.O.I., R.E.*, organised by the Ipswich Art Club and Ipswich Borough Council, 1985, p.13.
3. Quote taken from Webber, M., Introduction to the Retrospective Exhibition catalogue for *Anna Airy, R.I., R.O.I, R.E.*, organised by the Ipswich Art Club and Ipswich Borough Council, 1985, p.7.
4. The Melvill Nettleship Prize for Figure Composition was founded in 1897 by the mother of Henry Nettleship, a former student in the Slade School of Fine Art, in his memory.
5. Beattie-Crozier, G., Anna Airy: My adventures with brush and palette, *Pearsons Magazine,* October 1924, p.205.
6. ibid., p.205.
7. Information from the *Catalogue of Paintings and Drawings by Anna Airy, R.I., R.O.I., R.E.,* May-July, 1930, Harrogate Corporation Art Gallery. This exhibition was the first to be held in the new gallery.
8. Hardie, M., ibid.
9. The founder members of the Pastel Society included Frank Brangwyn, Laurence Whistler, G.F. Watts and Auguste Rodin. The Royal Society of Painters and Etchers was established in 1880 and the Royal Institute of Painters in Watercolours was founded in 1882 with membership open to those artists who have shown work of a consistently high standard in its annual exhibition.
10. The Carfax & Co. Gallery was founded in 1899 by William Rothenstein and John Fothergill.
11. Hardie, M., ibid., p.1-2.
12. Anna Airy Drawings of fruit, flowers and foliage, *International Studio,* Vol. 55, March-June 1915, p.189-195.
13. Rimbault-Dibdin, E., *Catalogue of paintings and drawings by Anna Airy, R.I., R.O.I., R.E.,* May-July, 1930, Harrogate Corporation Art Gallery.
14. Beattie-Crozier, G., ibid., p.292.
15. Information from the Ipswich Art Club Archives.
16. Beattie-Crozier, G., ibid., p.289-290.
17. Harries, M., and Harries, S., *The War Artists* (In association with the Imperial War Museum and the Tate Gallery), Michael Joseph Ltd., 1983., p.162.
18. Information from the Centenary Exhibition of the Ipswich Art Club, 1974 catalogue.
19. Bradford Arts Jubilee, *Yorkshire Observer,* March 1952.
20. Information from the Ipswich Art Club Archives.

LEFT:
Gay Glitter in June, date unknown, oil on canvas, 89 x 120cm, reproduced by kind permission of Newport Museum and Art Gallery.

RIGHT:
Hawker's Noon Day, 1927, (detail), oil on canvas, 127 x 152cm
© Bonhams London, UK/The Bridgeman Art Library.

CHAPTER TWO:
ANNA AIRY: FIRST WORLD WAR ARTIST

Anna Airy was at the height of her career during the early part of the 20th century with work in various galleries, memberships of prestigious art societies, work illustrated in the Studio publication and continual acceptance to the annual Royal Academy of Arts Summer Exhibition in London. Her work covered a wide range of themes and subjects: she was as comfortable with a still life as she was with a formal portrait. Her figurative work, showing her outstanding draughtsmanship, particularly of figures within interiors, brought her great acclaim. Not many female artists at that time could boast the same level of success.

Her night-time investigations and drawings made in the slums by the River Thames, whilst a student at the Slade School of Fine Art, influenced one aspect of her work: a desire to capture the lives of working- class people. Typical examples were *The Gambling Club* (1913), *The Wine Shop* and *The Rights of Man* (1917). These large formal works, shown at the important exhibitions, were described by one journalist as being 'saloon bar art'.1 It was noted, however, that this type of work brought her both recognition from the Royal Academy and more importantly, led to selection by the Canadian War Records Office and the British   War Memorials Committee during the First World War. Airy also took part in several First World War fundraising activities, such as the War Relief Exhibition in aid of the Red Cross and St. John Ambulance Society and the Artists' General Benevolent Institution in 1915 at the Royal Academy of Arts, where she exhibited the etching, *The Cast of Dice.* Two years later she showed eight works, including *The Barn, Willow Pattern* and *Thief's Rewarded,* at the Winter Exhibition of Graphic Art in aid of the Red Cross and St. John Ambulance Society.2

In 1916 the Canadian Government decided that their country's involvement in the First World War should be recorded for history through paintings, drawings and sculptures. This task was given to the Canadian War Records Office, based in London, under the management of Canadian-born Lord Beaverbrook, owner of the *Daily Express* newspaper. In 1917, Sir Edmund Walker, Chairman of the National Gallery

Board of Trustees in Canada, was appointed a member of the Canadian War Memorials Fund Committee with the task of commissioning 33 artists to record the general activities in 18 separate categories, such as Ship Battles, Infantry, Hospitals, Munitions and Aircraft. Selected artists included Edward Wadsworth, David Bomberg, William Rothenstein, John Lavery, Charles Ginner and William Roberts. Airy, alongside Clare Atwood, Laura Knight and Major Ambrose McEvoy, was designated the Training of Soldiers and Leave Scenes category. 3 Both Airy and Knight visited the Reserve camp of the 156th Canadian Infantry Battalion at Witley, in   Surrey. Airy produced a large canvas, *Cook-house at Witley Camp,* whilst Knight's work featured an open- air boxing match, *Physical Training (Boxing) at Witley Camp.* The two works were exhibited at the Canadian War Memorials Exhibition at the Royal Academy of Arts from January to February, 1919. After the exhibition the whole collection of paintings was transported back to Canada and exhibited in New York, Montreal and Toronto. Airy's painting was shown in Canada in 1919 alongside artists such as Frank Brangwyn, Harold Gilman and Laura Knight and later, amongst a total of two hundred works, at the National Gallery of Canada, in Ottawa, in 1924. According to a Canadian exhibition catalogue almost every British artist of note was employed, together with as many Canadians as were available. 4

The first British foray into war art, initially to be used for propaganda purposes, was set up by the British Government in 1916. It soon developed into a more artistic endeavour to record Britain's war effort. The Department of Information, established in 1917, was taken over by the Ministry of Information in 1918. Lord Beaverbrook was appointed Minister of Information. In 1916 the British Government had set up the first official war artists' scheme. *"It's often misunderstood what the role of the war artist is. A lot of people think it is frontline sketching. War art encompasses far more than battle scenes or life at the frontline – it is about artists' creative responses to all aspects of war as seen and experienced by ordinary people, civilians, as well as servicemen and women."* 5

The British War Memorials Committee (BWMC), established by Lord Beaverbrook and Arnold Bennett, wanted to have complete control over all aspects of this project, from the choice of artists to listing the subject areas to be covered.

LEFT:
The Cast of Dice, 1914,
etching, 56 x 40cm. Exhibited at the Liverpool Autumn Exhibition, 1914.

Cookhouse, Witley Camp, 1917,
oil on canvas, © Canadian War Museum, Ottawa, Canada.

The catalogue for the Canadian War Memorials
Exhibition, 1919, noted: *"Here is portrayed an
amusing scene of army life in a Reserve camp. The
painting is not without that touch of humour which is
rarely absent from Airy's work, as may be noted by the
action of the figure in the foreground. The interior is of a
regional cook-house at Witley Camp, Surrey, in 1917.
At the time, the 156th Canadian Infantry Battalion
was at the training camp."*

They also took the decision to separate the list into two: Home Front and the Western Front. The Home Front artists could incorporate those excluded from the battle zone, such as women and older men, who could still have an opportunity to be involved. Eight groups were suggested: Land, Munitions, Merchant Marine, Army, Air Force, Navy, Public Manifestations and Clerical and other Work for Women. Those artists sent abroad included Augustus John, John Nash, Paul Nash, Henry Lamb, Henry Tonks, William Orpen, William Roberts, Wyndham Lewis, Stanley Spencer and George Clausen. The British War Memorials Committee extended the number of artists commissioned to include three women, Anna Airy, Flora Lion and Dorothy Coke, but none of the work was accepted.[6]

Airy was commissioned by the BWMC to produce a painting depicting munitions girls. Arrangements were made for the artist to be given a permit to visit a munitions factory in Enfield in London to *obtain sketches for the purpose of painting a picture entitled 'Munitions Girls' for the Ministry of Information.* [7] A verbal agreement was made with Paul Konody, the influential art critic for *The Observer* and *The Daily Mail* before the First World War, regarding the proposed size of canvas, 125" x 72", and a fee of £300 plus expenses to be paid. Shortly after Airy had started to develop the work she received a letter stating that the size of the canvas should have been 5 x 3 ft, enclosing a payment of £150. [8] This last-minute change put the artist into a rage and she soon wrote back stating: *"I have been in communication with Paul Konody, and he upholds me that a definite commission, as above was placed - and I must remind you that the custom of the artists' profession is to place commissions by word of mouth, not in writing: this custom dates back to the time of Sir Joshua Reynolds ... Any decision to break with this arrangement made without the knowledge of your own art advisor to the scheme and without consulting me in the slightest is perfectly indefensible."* [9]

Alfred Yockney, previously associated with London art galleries and appointed Secretary of the BWMC from February 1918, wrote to reassure Airy about the situation and she started the painting again, accepting a fee of £150. According to the correspondence, the work was in progress by February 1919 and completed and ready for inspection in May. Airy submitted a description of the work to the committee: *"A crowd of London girls leaving the press-house of a shell factory. On the right are the piles of shell cases which they have manufactured and which are waiting to go on to the machine–shops to be turned, the gasometer like structure in the background provides the meter pressure to work the presses that make the shell-cases and the girls regulate the presses and propel the red-hot billets from the furnace to the press. The London girls, however long and hard they work, are always laughing."* [10]

A few days later Airy was informed that the painting did not appeal to the Committee. They felt that the work looked unfinished and it was even suggested that something could be done to make the picture more successful from their point of view.[11] Her response was not surprising: *"I am sorry that the committee does not like the picture. I am afraid that I cannot do more to better it, or I should have done so before I sent it in!"* [12] Shortly afterward, she wrote to the Committee informing them that she had decided to destroy the work, stating to Alfred Yockney: *"it will shortly be found in pieces in the dust bin."* [13]

Running concurrently was another, more important commission, from the Munitions Committee of the Imperial War Museum (IWM). In April 1918 it was suggested that she should paint six large canvases for preservation in the Imperial War Museum. Eventually, it was decided that she would produce four pictures representing typical scenes in munitions' factories and a formal contract was made between the Imperial War Museum Committee and Anna Airy, dated 27th June 1918. This contract dictated to the artist the places the artist should work, the titles and size of the work, media to be used and, unlike her male counterparts, imposed strict terms of employment with a right to refuse the work and not pay for it.[14] Furthermore the agreement stated that all four paintings should be completed and ready for inspection before November 1919, with two works completed by January 1919. Airy would be paid £280 per painting, as well as all costs and expenses including travel and lodgings. If all the work was not completed, the fee diminished by 5% per month. Additionally the IWM had exclusive copyright to the works.

Undeterred by these restrictions, Airy set about producing four large-scale canvases, each highlighting a key area of British arms manufacturing. These works were much more of a challenge, both physically and artistically, than her first commission for Canada. The situation was a far cry from her studio in London, where she had total artistic control: at these places she was observing people working in very basic and often dangerous conditions. Perhaps, however, after her early student escapades, this did not bother her at all.

Over the year Airy travelled across the country to capture workers preparing for war in munitions' factories in London, Manchester and Glasgow. The four paintings, with the first suggested titles, were: *Assembly Shop at the Aircraft Manufacturing Co., Hendon; The "L" press forging an 18" gun at the works of Messrs. Armstrong Whitworth & Co's. Works at Openshaw; 15" Shell Shop at Singer's, Glasgow* and *The Shell Forge - Hackney Marshes, London*.15 An artist of her experience and calibre was able to adapt quickly to conditions which required her to work very quickly to capture the various activities, the colours of the red-hot metal, and to deal with oil paints which dried rapidly in the heat. Airy enjoyed the camaraderie of working with the men and women in the factories. They were interested in her work and looked after her. At the Hackney Marshes they rigged up a shelter for her out of a piece of corrugated iron: *"but red hot shells would be rolled right against my screen - which acted like an oven, with me inside. Often too the shelter would fall over and send me and my easel flying - then they'd rush round and pick us up again!"* 16

Airy successfully completed the four canvases, which captured the manufacturing process and the conditions in which the people worked. The viewpoints that she chose added further to the drama of the paintings, as did the colours she used. Airy finally delivered her four paintings in July 1919, within the contracted date.17 Furthermore, she produced a fifth canvas, *Women Working in a Gas Retort House, South Metropolitan Gas Company, London,* at about the same time. This painting joined Airy's four other works at the Imperial War Museum. It had been commissioned by the Women's Work Sub-Committee, established by Lady Norman. She was the daughter of Lord Aberconway, and wife of M.P. Sir Henry Norman, who had supported the creation of the IWM in 1917, and was one of its trustees. In 1917 Lady Norman became Chair of the Women's Work Sub-Committee, responsible for recording the work of women during the war. After it was decided that women artists should not go to the Front but should instead record activities on the home front, they commissioned nine women artists, including Airy.

With the outbreak of the Second World War, the War Artists Advisory Committee, under the Chairmanship of Sir Kenneth Clark, considered over 800 names for the role of war artists. Unfortunately, the First World War artists, who had made such an important contribution to the scheme, including Anna Airy, Stanhope Forbes, George Clausen and several others, were rejected.18 Working independently, Airy produced one painting, *The Hall of Lincoln's Inn, 1944 during restoration from Enemy Action,* and this was exhibited at the Royal Academy of Arts Summer Exhibition in 1945. After the Second World War, Airy continued her artistic endeavours as well as becoming more involved with the Ipswich Art Club, where she became President in 1945.

FOOTNOTES:
1. Ferraby, H.C., Saloon Bar Art: A Woman Painter's Adventures, *John O' London's Weekly,* December 1920.
2. Information from the Royal Academy Collections: *www.racollection.org.uk.*
3. Temple of War Art: Canada's Great Memorial, 40 Huge Decorative Paintings, Works by 33 Artists, *Sunday Pictorial,* 21st December 1918.
4. Information from the National Gallery of Canada exhibition catalogue: *Second Exhibition of Canadian War Memorials,* 1924. p.7.
5. Palmer, K., *Women War Artists,* Tate Publishing, 2012.
6. Harries, M., and Harries, S., *The War Artists,* (In association with the Imperial War Museum and the Tate Gallery), Michael Joseph Ltd., 1983, p.90.
7. Letter from Major C.S.Paulet, Ministry of Munitions, to Alfred Yockney, Ministry of Information, 9th May 1918, (IWM War Artists Archive, 'Miss Anna Airy' 1918-1959 ART/WA1/031).
8. Letter sent to Anna Airy, probably by Alfred Yockney, dated 27th September,1918. (IWM War Artists Archive, 'Miss Anna Airy' 1918-1959 ART/WA1/031).
9. Quote from a letter from Anna Airy to Alfred Yockney, dated 4th October 1918. (IWM War Artists Archive, 'Miss Anna Airy' 1918-1959 ART/WA1/031).
10. Information from a letter from Anna Airy to Alfred Yockney, 25th May, 1919. (IWM War Artists Archive, 'Miss Anna Airy' 1918-1959 ART/WA1/031).
11. Letter from Alfred Yockney to Anna Airy, 28th May,1919. (IWM War Artists Archive, 'Miss AnnaAiry' 1918-1959 ART/WA1/031).
12. Letter from Anna Airy to Alfred Yockney, 30th May,1919. (IWM War Artists Archive, 'Miss Anna Airy' 1918-1959 ART/WA1/031).
13. Letter from Anna Airy to Alfred Yockney, 12th June 1919. (IWM War Artists Archive, 'Miss Anna Airy' 1918-1959 ART/WA1/031).
14. A copy of the contract is held in the archives of Anna Airy at the Imperial War Museum. (IWM War Artists Archive, 'Miss Anna Airy' 1918-1959 ART/WA1/031).
15. A proposed painting of the Chilwell factory was replaced by one of the Singer Factory in Glasgow. (IWM War Artists Archive, 'Miss Anna Airy' 1918-1959 ART/WA1/031).
16. Beattie-Crozier, G., Anna Airy: My adventures with brush and palette, *Pearson's Magazine,* October 1924, p.294-295.
17. Airy also produced an etching of the Shell Forge in 1919.
18. Harries, M., and Harries, S., ibid., p.162.

The following descriptions of each painting, with Airy's original titles shown in brackets, were requested by the Committee. After Airy submitted her descriptions some slight editorial changes were made.

The Verdun Shop, 15-inch shells: Singer Manufacturing Co., Clydebank, Glasgow, 1918, oil on canvas, 182 x 217cm, *(15" Shell Shop at Singer's Glasgow).*

This painting was exhibited at the Royal Academy of Arts Summer Exhibition in 1919. © Imperial War Museums (IWM ART 2271).

Anna Airy recorded: "In this large shop, turning and banding with copper, 15" shells. Although doing very heavy work, the shop is staffed entirely by women, under a foreman. A derrick has been arranged to each machine so that there is no unnecessary waiting, but a shell may be handled without delay by two of the girls. Each shell has its own little wooden bogey to run it about the shop. Some of the shells have their copper bands on, some have not. P38 in front has come back for some slight adjustment. On the floor is a cap which is screwed into the end of the shell."

The Shell Forge: National Projectile Factory,
Hackney Marshes, London, 1918,
oil on canvas, 182 x 217cm. (*The Shell Forge - Hackney Marshes).*

This painting was exhibited at the Royal Academy of Arts Summer Exhibition in 1919. © Imperial War Museums (IWM ART 4032).

Anna Airy recorded that: "This picture shows the progress of a steel billet from the furnace to the machine shop. On the left of the picture the billet is seen red-hot from the furnace, grasped by the tongs that have guided it to the press, which, worked by hydraulic pressure and controlled by the girl standing at the lever, has punched a hole on the red-hot billet, making it into a hollow shell case. The nose of the punch is seen to be still hot from its work. The shell case is now toppled out of the tongs onto the ground and is rolled to the gauger in front, who is seen in the picture testing the shell with a wall-gauge, which is done with extraordinary quickness and certainty. This being done, a boy with a puddling rod runs the hot shell case away to cool, as is seen in the middle of the picture. On the right is a party of men lifting the cooled-off shell cases with double tongs onto the bogey on the line which runs them to the stack in the yard outside, whence they will shortly go to the machine shop to be turned. This process was continually repeated day and night at the presses down the length of this house."

*Forging the Jacket for an 18" gun at Messrs.
Armstrong-Whitworth & Co's Works at Openshaw,
1918,*
oil on canvas, 182 x 217cm.
*(The "L" Press forging an 18-inch gun at the works of Messrs.
Armstrong- Whitworth & Co., at Openshaw).*

This painting was exhibited at the Royal Academy of
Arts Summer Exhibition in 1919. © Imperial War
Museums (IWM ART 2272).

Anna Airy recorded: "Here is depicted one portion
(the jacket) of the heavy 18" Naval Gun about to be
forged in the hydraulic press. It has just been drawn
from the furnace on the right of the picture and the
mass of red hot metal weighs 60 tons. A long mandrel
is inserted into the billet (which has already been
roughly forged and bored through the centre) while it
lies in the furnace, and the great crane working on the
beams overhead, at the top of the picture, gently
withdraws the whole mass. In the picture, the red-hot
billet has arrived at the press, and the small figure of a
man will be seen in front of it directing another man
behind the press which way the crane (in the
background above) must be ordered to work in order
to swing the tail of the mandrel, so that the hot
forging may be exactly in the right position for the
press to work on it. The huge press works on the metal
quite gently though with enormous force, and when
raised again, the watchful crane above is ready to turn
the forging slightly for another squeeze. In the front of
this picture stands the foreman of the shop watching
the process put through. The foremost crane above is
busy shackling on to the next billet which has been
run into the shop on a truck, by a railway engine
along the lines in front."

An Aircraft Assembly Shop, Hendon, 1918,
oil on canvas, 182 x 217cm, *(Assembly Shop at the Aircraft
Manufacturing Co. Hendon)* © Imperial War Museums (IWM
ART 1931).

Airy commented that: "This canvas shows the interior
of one of the erecting shops in an aeroplane factory.
The men and women at the benches are engaged on
the various details required to render the bodies seen
on the left fit to be run up the ramp at the back of the
shop into the upper shop on the right of the picture,
where the machines receive their necessary fittings and
where the stripes and circles of red, white and blue,
denominating a British machine, are painted on -
together with the individual number of each
machine."

Women working in a Gas Retort House, South Metropolitan Gas Company, London, 1918,
oil on canvas, 182 x 217cm. © Imperial War Museums
(IWM ART 2852).

CHAPTER THREE
ANNA AIRY AND THE IPSWICH ART CLUB

The Ipswich Fine Art Club, established in 1874, is one of the earliest art clubs to be formed in Britain and still running today.1 Set up by Edward Packard and John Duvall, a committee was soon elected and club rules established. The Club held its first exhibition at the Old Lecture Hall in Tower Street, Ipswich in 1875. Through its annual exhibitions the Club promoted the work of many painters, sculptors and printmakers, both amateur and professional, as well as contributing to the cultural life of Suffolk.

The original logo for the Ipswich Fine Art Club

The popularity of the annual exhibitions prompted the committee to consider the need for their own premises and a lease was purchased on land next to Ipswich Museum on the High Street. The new gallery, opened in 1880, was ready for the Club's sixth annual exhibition of members' work. The Club also organised separate exhibitions, including a major show of work by Thomas Gainsborough in 1927. Membership has included many of the most important East Anglian artists of their day, such as Harry Becker, Edward Smythe, Colin Moss, Sir Alfred Munnings, Leonard Squirrell and Edward Seago, some of whom played an important role in the running of the Club. 2

LEFT:
The Kitchen's Queen, 1911,
oil on canvas, 110 x 85cm
Shown at the Royal Academy of Arts Summer Exhibition in 1911 and at the Ipswich Fine Art Club Annual Exhibition in 1921.
By kind permission of Colchester and Ipswich Museum Services.

In her childhood and youth, Airy spent time at the family home in Playford, near Ipswich. Her aunt Annot, who had helped to raise her, had work accepted by the Club between 1882 and 1895 and her cousin, Arthur Langton Airy, was a member of the Ipswich Fine Art Club.3 This is probably where the connection between Airy and the Ipswich Art Club began. According to published records, Airy became a member of the Club in 1903, at the age of about twenty-one, but there are no records of her submitting work to the Annual Exhibition until 1921. This first work, The Kitchen's Queen, now in the collection of Colchester and Ipswich Museums, had been shown ten years earlier at the Royal Academy of Arts Summer Exhibition. Airy continued to submit work to the Club's Annual Exhibition for many years. By 1933, she and her husband had moved to the family home in Playford. They settled down and he became well known in the village, while she continued to work from her purpose-built studio in the cottage,

BELOW: *Clothed figure in action,*
pencil on paper. From Airy, A., *Making a Start in Art,* The Studio Publications, 1951, p.76.

keeping herself to herself. As was her practice in London, she employed the local villagers to pose for her, as well as her maid and groups of local boys. In 2014 one elderly man recalled having to pose for Airy as though he were climbing a wall and on another occasion he posed biting into an apple. The local boys were paid for the length of time they posed and how they behaved: usually half-a-crown a day. 4

This idyllic life in rural Suffolk was temporarily halted after Airy heard that the warehouse in London which contained her works had been badly damaged during the Blitz. Airy had to wait for several days to

A study for *Spring is in the Garden,* pastel on paper, reproduced in Airy, A., *The Art of Pastel,* Winsor and Newton, 1930, Plate III.

hear if her work, like that of several other artists, had been destroyed. Fortunately it had, on the whole, survived intact. After the work was returned to her in Playford she decided that it would be a good idea to exhibit the collection and approached the Ipswich Art Club Committee for advice. *"Owing to the London Blitz, I have here the whole of my work, doing nothing. Merely to give an idea of what I could provide - I could hang the Wolsey Gallery: large oils, watercolours, drawings and etchings and I could make an important show. Would your Ipswich Art Club care to sponsor, as it were such as*

exhibition, upon terms such as have been accorded me for the various one man shows I have given in London: an agreed percentage on sales?" 5

After much negotiation the exhibition took place in the Wolsey Gallery at Christchurch Mansion in Ipswich in 1943. Not only did it prove very popular with the general public, but it also raised the artist's profile in Suffolk. At the Annual General Meeting in 1945, Lord Ullswater, the President, who had decided to step down, proposed that Anna Airy be elected as the new President of Ipswich Art Club. Airy thus became the first female President in the Club's history and was held in great regard by members, not least because she was a professional artist of international repute. Airy always set herself high standards in her work and her main objective for the Club was to raise the standards of the members' work and of the Annual Exhibition. To this end a stricter selection process was instigated and the decision was taken to have fewer works on display.6 David Thompson, art critic and previous Chairman of the Club, commented: *"There were few areas of the Club's activities which were not influenced by her enthusiastic interest and support. A powerful and commanding figure, she was a frequent and outspoken critic of much of what she called 'modern art'. She was impatient with anything which fell outside the standards of draughtsmanship and skill she set herself."*7

Whilst Airy had very strong opinions about modern art, which she later expressed in her book, 'Making a Start in Art' (1951), one thing that was very important to her was the encouragement of young artists. An early sign of this came about during the late 1950s when it was suggested that young artists or art students, aged between seventeen and twenty-two, and living in Suffolk, should be invited to submit work to the Annual Exhibition. The suggested prizes were for First place 10 guineas, Second place five guineas and three guineas for Third place. According to the Club minutes, the first young artists' competition took place in 1958. In 1961 Paul Reeve was awarded first prize, Gareth Jones second place and third place went to Margaret Fox.8 A year later Airy wrote to Gareth Jones giving him advice: *"the sending-in day for the Royal Institute of Oil Painters (ROI) show this year will be I think October 1st and you had better write for form & labels in good time and select, say a couple of medium or fair-sized works. If your work is hung, let me know without delay, and I will suggest that your name go onto the list of candidates for election and I will propose you. We can find a necessary seconder nearer the election date."*9

Earth's Ministers, c.1930,
oil on canvas, 75 x 60cm.
This painting features farmers from Playford including M. Philips (left), Walter Dunnet (centre) and Fred Dunnett (behind central group, looking sideways). Shown at the Royal Academy of Arts Summer Exhibition in 1930.
By kind permission of Mr C. Lofts.

The minutes of the Annual General Meeting for the following year recorded that a competition of this sort: *"should enable the club to catch young people, which we must have if the club is to go forward. Young people must be encouraged, in what they are feeling, what they are thinking, we have got to look at how they express themselves and what sort of feelings they express. Art is a personal feeling differing from a past generation. You have to be careful and encourage your artists of real promise."*[10]

A sub-committee was established to explore how to develop the idea of a students' competition to encourage younger people to join the Club. All sorts of ideas were expressed at committee level, including electing young artists as associate members to the Club and considering art materials as prizes. They also decided not to award if the work was not to a sufficient standard and only the winners and recommended work should be hung. Following the death of Anna Airy in October 1964, the Committee established The Anna Airy Memorial Fund to raise money to support an award for young artists. In the same year, The Anna Airy Award Competition was opened to anyone under the age of twenty-five, maintaining the principle that prizes would not be awarded if the standard was not high enough.[11] Two years later the Club published a document establishing the rules of the Anna Airy Memorial Award and noting that it was: *"instituted to perpetuate the memory of a distinguished and much respected President, the late Anna Airy, in gratitude for all she did for the Club and for the cause of art."* [12]

For many years, entries for the Anna Airy Award formed part of the Annual Exhibition. However, as this special award became more popular with young artists across the county, it was decided that it should be the focus of a special annual show. Since the mid-1990s the Anna Airy Award Exhibition has been staged in various venues across Ipswich. More recently, the exhibition has been held at University Campus Suffolk (UCS) and this has helped to attract a wider range of students, raising the standard of works submitted. Over the years several winners of the Award have gone on to establish themselves as professional artists and teachers, including Kate Reynolds, Tricia Newell, Jevan Watkins, Sula Rubens and Andrew Casey. The legacy of Anna Airy lives on through these young people who are just starting to explore their artistic potential, as Airy did in London over a century ago.

FOOTNOTES:

1. The word Fine was dropped from the Club's name in 1925. In 1993 the word *Society* replaced *Club*.
2. For more information on the history of the Club and its members see: Webber, M., Introduction to the *Centenary Exhibition of the Ipswich Art Club: 1874-1974.*
3. Annot Airy was born in Playford in 1844 and exhibited with the Ipswich Art Club between 1882 and 1895. Three watercolours by Christabel Airy, born in 1842, were displayed at the *Anna Airy R.I., R.O.I., R.E., Retrospective Exhibition,* in Ipswich in 1985. Her cousin Arthur Langton Airy also exhibited work at the Ipswich Fine Art Club between 1899-1912.
4. Author in conversation with Mr. Dunnett, April 2014.
5. A letter from Anna Airy to Mrs Lewcock, 7th August, 1943.
6. Information from the Ipswich Art Club Minute Book No.6, 1936 to 1945.
7. Thompson, D., *Ipswich Art Society 1974-1999,* Ipswich Art Society, 1999.
8. Information from the minutes of the Ipswich Art Club Committee meeting, August 1961.
9. Information from a letter from Anna Airy to Gareth Jones, 27th April 1962. Courtesy of Gareth Jones.
10. Information from the minutes of the Ipswich Art Club, March 1964.
11. Information from the minutes of the Ipswich Art Club, November 1964.
12. Information from the Anna Airy Award Application form.

ANNA AIRY AWARD WINNERS:

The following list has been collated using several sources including the Ipswich Art Club Archives. Any omissions relating to particular years may indicate either that no information is available or that no award was given in that year.

1968	Stephen Todd	1990	Andrew Casey
1969	Linda Spendley	1992	Amanda Bell
1971	Terry Moore	1993	Jevan Watkins
1972	David Jay	1994	Desmond Brett
1973	Michael Hall	1995	Andrew Luetchford
1974	David Jay	1996	Matthew Derbyshire
1975	Stephen Todd	1998	Edward Parkinson
1976	Tricia Newell	2000	Dominic Peach
1977	Tricia Newell	2001	Sheri Cannell
1978	John Baldry	2003	Alistair Campbell
1979	Jean Ketcher	2004	Laura McElhinney
1980	Tricia Newell	2005	Adam Weal
1981	Julie Adams/John Baldry	2006	Chloe Sage
1982	A.W. Thorpe	2007	Polyanna Jackson
1983	Kate Reynolds	2008	Georgina Slais-Jones
1984	Julie Adams	2009	Velvet Stratford Wright
1985	Cathie Shuttleworth	2010	Abigail Whittaker
1986	Cathie Shuttleworth	2012	Polly Johnston
1987	Rachel Green	2013	Sophie Edwards
1989	Sula Rubens		

ANDREW CASEY

I first entered my artwork into the Ipswich Art Society Summer exhibition in 1985 just after leaving college. This was the first time I had put work into a show and attended a private view of any kind. I was really excited to gain third prize. During that summer Evangeline Dickson asked me to write a review of the Anna Airy exhibition at the Christchurch Mansion which was my first piece of journalism. I was elected to the Ipswich Art Club Committee in 1986 and was later involved in setting up the Anna Airy Award exhibition. Winning the award in 1990, just before my 25th birthday, boosted my confidence and encouraged me to pursue art which I did through my Young Blood group of artists.

KATE REYNOLDS

As I recall, I was between college courses, at home after three years attending Brighton Polytechnic, studying for a BA in 3D design and about to embark on an MA degree in ceramics in Cardiff… so 1983. I was encouraged by my father to enter some work into the annual exhibition and submit it for the Anna Airy Award competition. At this time in the IAS history, there were very few new graduates and not many young artists joining the Society. I therefore had a good chance to win a prize.

I submitted three shallow bowls containing engraved self-portraits made on the wheel, using a dark chocolate brown clay which I had glazed with a white tin glaze and then engraved and painted oxides on each one. I was surprised to win first prize and very encouraged to be accepted as a new member of the society. It was a great boost at the start of my art career in East Anglia. I continued to enjoy exhibiting with the IAS for many years afterwards.

SULA RUBENS

To be awarded the Anna Airy Award twice, shortly after my degree at St. Martin's, was immensely encouraging. I remember, both times, that I spent it on materials which I used for three-month landscape painting trips to Northern Spain and to the Spanish Pyrenees. I made a lot of paintings during those trips.

TOP: Andrew Casey
The Woman, 2012.

CENTRE: Kate Reynolds
Tall noble head, 2012.

BOTTOM: Sula Rubens
The Cricketer, 2013.

A portrait study of the late H. B. Irving, c.1916,
reproduced in Airy, A., *Making a Start in Art,* Studio Publication,
1951, p.59.

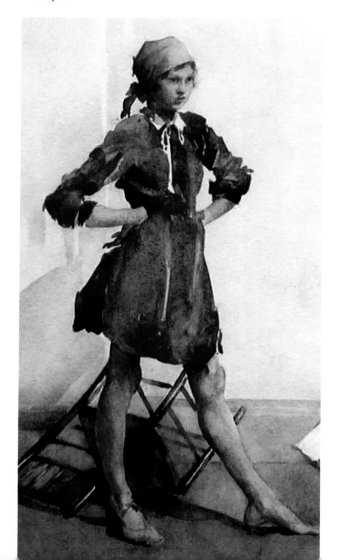

ANNA AIRY SOLO EXHIBITIONS:
Carfax & Co. Gallery, London, 1907
Paterson's Gallery, London, 1911
Fine Art Society, London, 1915, 1920
Anna Airy, Christchurch Mansion, Ipswich, 1943
Anna Airy: Paintings, Drawings and Prints, Royal Society of British Artists, 1952
Anna Airy: Retrospective exhibition, New Gallery, Ipswich, 1965
Anna Airy R.I., R.O.I., R.E., Retrospective Exhibition, Ipswich Art Club and Ipswich Borough Council, Christchurch Mansion, Ipswich, 1985

EXHIBITIONS:
Royal Academy of Arts Summer Exhibition, London, 1905-1956 (not 1931)
Franco-British Exhibition, London, 1908
Liverpool Autumn Exhibition, 1908-1911, 1913-1915, 1926-1927, 1930, 1933-1935
New English Art Club, 1909-1913
British Pavilion, Venice Biennale, 1912
International Exhibition of Fine Art, Rome, 1912
War Relief Exhibition in aid of the Red Cross and St. John Ambulance Society and the Artists' General Benevolent Institution, Royal Academy of Arts, London, 1915
International Exhibition of Fine Art, Rome, 1915
Winter Exhibition of Graphic Art in aid of the Red Cross and St. John Ambulance Society, Royal Academy of Arts, London, 1917
War Pictures, Royal Academy of Arts, 1919
Canadian War Memorials Exhibition, Royal Academy of Arts, London, 1919
A group of foreign paintings from the Carnegie International Exhibition, The Art Institute of Chicago, 1920
Ipswich Art Club, Ipswich 1921-1964
Exhibition at the Art Institute of Chicago, 1920
Royal Society of Portrait Painters, Royal Academy of Arts, 1921
Canadian National Exhibition: Paintings by British and Canadian Artists and International Graphic Art, Toronto, 1921
Canadian National Exhibition: Paintings and Sculpture by British, American and Canadian Artists and International Graphic Art and photography, Toronto, 1924
Second Exhibition of Canadian War Memorials, National Gallery of Canada, 1924
Paintings by British and Canadian Artists and later Graphic Art and Photography, Toronto, 1924
Summer Exhibition of Modern Art, Doncaster Museum, 1925-1940 (not 1926, 1930- 1932)
International Exhibition, New Zealand, 1926
British Empire Trade Exhibition, Buenos Aires, 1931
Empire Exhibition Scotland, 1938
War Paintings Exhibition, Art Exhibitions Bureau, 1940 (location unknown)
Aid to Russia Exhibition, Wallace Collection, 1942
Royal Glasgow Institute of Fine Arts, 1949, 1955
Norwich Festival of Britain, 1951
Art Exhibitions Bureau, Industrial Britain Exhibition, London, 1955

AWARDS:
Melvill Nettleship Prize 1900, 1901 and 1902
Professor Thane's prize for Anatomy
Slade School Scholarship, 1901
Place of Honour at the International Exhibition of Fine Art, Rome, 1912

The Termagant (detail),
watercolour, 48 x 66cm., By kind permission of Cheffins, Auctioneers, Cambridge.

Youth, 1926, oil on canvas, 76 x101cm, shown at the Royal
Academy of Arts Summer Exhibition in 1926.

RIGHT: A study for the *Youth* canvas, pastel on paper,
reproduced in Airy, A., *The Art of Pastel,* Winsor and Newton, 1930, p.12.

WORK EXHIBITED AT THE ROYAL ACADEMY OF ARTS SUMMER EXHIBITION

1905 Michael Lee Esq.: Indian Mutiny

1906 The Right Hon. Sir J. Gorell Barnes, L.L.D. ; Willow Pattern

1907 La Penseuse

1908 For Carnival "For my gold is turned to silver, and my silver's turned to brass."

1909 The Scandalmongers

1910 High Noon is Passing

1911 The Kitchen's Queen

1912 The Expert Player; Portion of Scripture

1913 The Gambling Club

1914 St. Stephen's, Walbrook, E.C; The Braggart

1915 Mid-day in a City Church; Richard Whiteing Esq.; The Tale-bearer

1916 Pauline, elder daughter of P.G. Kennedy Esq.; "Autumn treads where Summer rains"

1917 "Rights of Man"; Alexander the Waiter: his Corner; H.B. Irving Esq.

1918 Error in Pay

1919 The "L" Press forging an 18-in gun at the works of Messrs. Armstrong-Whitworth & Openshaw; The "Verdun" shop, 15-in shells: Singer Manufacturing & Co., Clydebank, Glasgow; The Shell Forge: National Projectile Factory, Hackney Marshes, E. London

1920 Roses Triumphant; "Pay or Quit"

1921 On the Border-line; Patricia, daughter of G. Baldwin Hamilton Esq. in her grandmother's gown

1922 In the Stable; June Morning

1923 The Flower Shop

1924 Ripening

1925 Gardener's Boy; Morning-gathered

1926 A "First Night" Harvest; Youth; The Man with the Macaw

1927 Hawker's Noonday; Pale January

1928 Heartache Stairs; Between the Showers

1929 A Side-table; Spring Birthday

1930 Earth's Ministers; Embroidery

1932 The Fledgling; The Devotee

1933 Summer Riot "The Illustrated"-portrait group

1934 Reflections; Madonna's Handmaids

1935 July Piece

1936 Mirrored Summer; Spring Song

1937 Blackberry Harvest

1938 Message of May

1939 The Vase

1940 August Keepsake

1941 Reflected Glory

1942 Winter Hedgerow

1943 New Year; Farewell

1944 Under the Apple tree

1945 The Hall of Lincoln's Inn, 1944, during restoration from enemy action

1946 The Rabbit Hole

1947 The Twisted Hedge Vine

1948 Ruined Root-knot

1949 The Silver Wreck

1950 Rustic Pillar

1952 Good Morning

1953 Jour de Fete; The Shadowed Water-splash

1954 Summer Glory; Leave-overs

1955 Spring Hedgerow

1956 Verdure and Decay

LEFT: *The Braggart*, 1914,
oil on canvas, 121 x 152cm.
Shown at the Royal Academy of Arts Summer Exhibition in 1914. © Bonhams London, UK/The Bridgeman Art Library.

BIOGRAPHICAL NOTES

GEORGE BIDDELL AIRY (1801-1892)

George Biddell Airy was born in Alnwick. He studied at elementary schools in Hereford and Colchester Grammar School. In 1819 he entered Trinity College, Cambridge, later elected scholar of Trinity. He graduated as senior wrangler and obtained first Smith's prize. In 1831 he was awarded the Copley medal of the Royal Society for these researches. In 1835 Airy was appointed Astronomer Royal. He was elected a Fellow of the Royal Society in 1836 and became President in 1871. He was five times president of the Royal Astronomical Society. In 1872 he was made KCB. In the same year he was nominated a Grand Cross in the Imperial Order of the Rose of Brazil; he also held the Prussian order "Pour le Mérite", and belonged to the Legion of Honour of France and to the Order of the North Star of Sweden and Norway. Sir George Airy resigned the office of Astronomer Royal in 1881.

GEOFFREY BUCKINGHAM POCOCK (1879–1960)

Born in London and educated at Merchant Taylors' School, then studied at the Slade School of Fine Art under P. Wilson and W.W. Russell, gaining first class certificates for painting and drawing and the Mason and Davis Prize. Freeman of Merchant Taylors' Company, and the City of London. He was a life master and teacher of etching at Battersea Polytechnic School of Art and later became life master for the London County Council School of Photo-Engraving and Lithography. He was Lieutenant East Yorkshire Regiment in the Boer War and received the Queen's South African Medal. In 1916 he married Anna Airy. He was known for his work in oils, watercolours, etchings and pastels. His work was exhibited at the Royal Academy of Arts Summer Exhibition from 1909 to 1936, as well as elsewhere in the UK.

WILFRID AIRY (1836-1925)

Born at the Royal Observatory in Greenwich, London, the fourth oldest child. He studied at Trinity, Cambridge from 1859. He became an apprentice with Robert Ransome, serving seven years at the Old Foundry and lodged at a house in Albion Hill. He qualified as an engineer. In 1881 he married Professor Listing's daughter. He was responsible for the scientific apparatus of Orwell Park Observatory. Airy edited his father's autobiography: *Sir George Biddle Airy KCB, Honorary Fellow of Trinity College, Cambridge, and Astronomer Royal from 1836 to 1881,* Cambridge University Press, 1896. Airy also wrote two books, including 'Iron Arches, The Practical Theory of the Continuous Arch', published by *Engineering* magazine, 1870.

TOP: *Siesta,* date unknown, watercolour. Reproduced by kind permission of the Mercer Art Gallery, Harrogate Borough Council.

CENTRE: A painting of farm buildings by Geoffrey Buckingham Pocock, oil on canvas, c.1920s. By kind permission of Mr C. Lofts.

BOTTOM: *Gardener's Boy,* 1925, oil on canvas, 40 x 50cm. Shown at the Royal Academy of Arts Summer Exhibition in 1925 and at the Ipswich Art Club Annual Exhibition in 1934.

BIBLIOGRAPHY:

BOOKS:

Airy, W. (Editor), *Sir George Biddle Airy KCB, Honorary Fellow of Trinity College, Cambridge and Astronomer Royal from 1836 to 1881,* University Press, 1896

Dunford, P., *A Biographical Dictionary of Women Artists in Europe and America since 1850,* Harvester and Wheatsheaf, 1990

Royal Academy Exhibitions 1905-1970, Vol. 1, E.P. Publishing, 1973

Foot, M.R.D., *Art and War, Twentieth Century Warfare as depicted by War Artists (In association with the Imperial War Museum),* Headline Books Publishing Ltd., 1990

Harries, M., and Harries, S., *War Artists, (In association with the Imperial War Museum and the Tate Gallery),* Michael Joseph Ltd., 1993

Palmer, K., *Women War Artists,* Tate Publishing, 2012

Chambers Biographical Dictionary, London, Chambers Harrap, 2007

Benezit Dictionary of British Graphic Artists and Illustrators, Volume 1, Oxford University Press, 2012

ARTICLES:

Anna Airy, Drawings of fruit, flowers and foliage, *International Studio,* Vol. 55, 1915

Varied work at the Fine Art Society, *Lady's Pictorial,* March 1915

Women Etchers of Today: Miss Anna Airy, *Lady's Pictorial,* February 1916

Temple of War Art: Canada's Great Memorial, 40 Huge Decorative Paintings, Works by 33 Artists, *Sunday Pictorial,* December 1918

Ferraby, H.C., Saloon Bar Art: A Woman Painter's Adventures, *John O'London's Weekly,* December 1920

Beattie-Crozier, G., Anna Airy: My adventures with brush and palette, *Pearson's Magazine,* October 1924

Miss Anna Airy, *East Anglian Daily Times,* October 1951

Bradford Arts Jubilee, *Yorkshire Observer,* March 1952

A Woman Artist's Jubilee Exhibition: Oils and Watercolours by Anna Airy, *The Illustrated London News,* October 1952

Akbar, A., Women at War: The female British artists who were written out of history, *The Independent,* April 2011

CATALOGUES:

Second Exhibition of Canadian War Memorials, National Gallery of Canada, 1924

Catalogue of Paintings and Drawings by Anna Airy, R.I., R.O.I., R.E., Harrogate Corporation Art Gallery, 1930

Anna Airy R.I., R.O.I., R.E. Paintings Drawings Prints, RBA Galleries, 1952, p.1-2

Centenary Exhibition of the Ipswich Art Club, 1974

Anna Airy, R.I., R.O.I., R.E., Ipswich Art Club, Ipswich Borough Council, 1985

Some Women Artists, Imperial War Museum, London, 1958-1959

ARCHIVES:

Imperial War Museum, London

Ipswich Museum and Galleries, Ipswich, Suffolk

Ipswich Art Society Archives

TOP: *Leave-overs,* date unknown, watercolour, 55 x 40cm. By kind permission of Cheffins, Auctioneers, Cambridge.

BOTTOM: *Autumn in a London Garden,* pastel, date unknown. Reproduced in: Airy, A., *The Art of Pastel,* Winsor and Newton, illustration 10, c.1930.

ACKNOWLEDGEMENTS

This book would not have been possible without the kind support and guidance of the many individuals, organisations and museums in this country and abroad who have supported the project from the start, not only giving me access to historical information but allowing me to use images of the artist's work. I would like to thank the following individuals: Stephen Cassidy, Derek Chambers, Chris Edmondson, Sue Slee, Gill Thomas and Jan Watson of the Ipswich Art Society sub-committee, for their support and encouragement; Adrian Parry, retired Honorary Secretary of the Ipswich Art Society, for allowing access to the Ipswich Art Society Archives; Paul Bruce for sharing his research, organising access to private archive material and introducing me to Mr. Lofts and Mr. Dunnett, who both knew Anna Airy.

I have visited many libraries and archives across the country and would like to thank the staff of The Imperial War Museum, Leeds City Art Library, and Woodbridge Library, for their help. Several museums, auction houses and private galleries were very generous in allowing me to use images from their collections. I would like to thank Susan Ross at the Canadian War Museum in Ottawa; Howard L. Rehs of the Rehs Gallery, New York; Neil McGregor, Museums Officer (Art and Exhibitions) Doncaster Museum & Art Gallery; Oliver Blackmore, Museum Curator, Newport Museum and Art Gallery, Wales; Dawn Heywood, Collections Access Officer at the Usher Gallery, Lincoln; Sarah Colegrave Fine Art, London; Emma Roodhouse and Theresa Calver from Colchester and Ipswich Museums; Jane Sellars, Mercer Art Gallery, Harrogate Borough Council; Bridgeman Art Library and Cheffins Auctioneers, Cambridge. Thanks are also due to the Royal Academy of Arts for helping me with my research.
I am indebted to the following people for their generous help: Molly Blum, Mary Burgess, John Harris, Eve Hostettler, Sally Pearson, Kate Reynolds and Sula Rubens. I would like to thank Diana MacMillan for commenting on my first draft of the book. Special thanks are due to Derek Chambers for his creative contribution to the book, his design expertise and his encouragement throughout the production process.
Andrew Casey

SPONSORS

Coes of Ipswich
Ipswich Decorative & Fine Arts Society
Ipswich Institute
John & Janet Murphy
Lamden Gallery, Ipswich
Notcutts Ltd, Woodbridge
Sabona Rheumatic Relief Co Ltd.
St. Mary's School, Cambridge
Willis Group, Ipswich

Mrs Telford Simpson, 1906,
oil on canvas, 66 x 66cm
By kind permission of Colchester
and Ipswich Museums Services.

Ipswich Art Society in association with University Campus Suffolk produced an exhibition of Anna Airy's work in 2014 and the publication of this book by Ipswich Art Society supported the exhibition.

RIGHT: A period photograph of Anna Airy, date unknown.